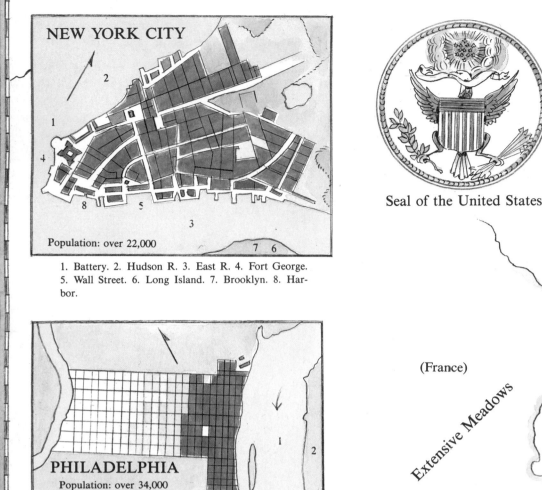

NEW YORK CITY

Population: over 22,000

1. Battery. 2. Hudson R. 3. East R. 4. Fort George.
5. Wall Street. 6. Long Island. 7. Brooklyn. 8. Harbor.

PHILADELPHIA
Population: over 34,000

1. Delaware River. 2. New Jersey.
After London, the second largest city in the English-speaking world.

CHARLESTON
Population: over 12,000

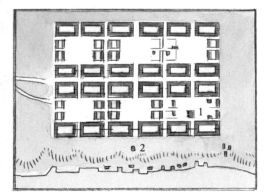

SAVANNAH
The first planned city in the United States.
1. Market. 2. Main Guard.

Seal of the United States

Lake Superior

*Northwest Territory
organized in 1787*

Outagamis

*Claimed by Massachusetts.
Ceded in 1785*

Lake Michigan

(France)

Extensive Meadows

Illinois R.

Fo

Wabash R.

For

Fort Gree

△ *Fort Vincennes (Sa*

Missouri R.

△ *Fort Kaskaskia*

Osage

LOUISIANA
(France)

Tennessee R.

Chickasaws

Mississippi R.

Indian Reserve by Proclamation, 1763

Nachees

Creek Country

Boundary by Royal Order, 1764

Choctaws

Boundary by Proclamation, 1763

*England gained con
Florida in 1763, bu
it back to Spain in*

WEST FLORIDA

New Orleans ●

Gulf of Mexico

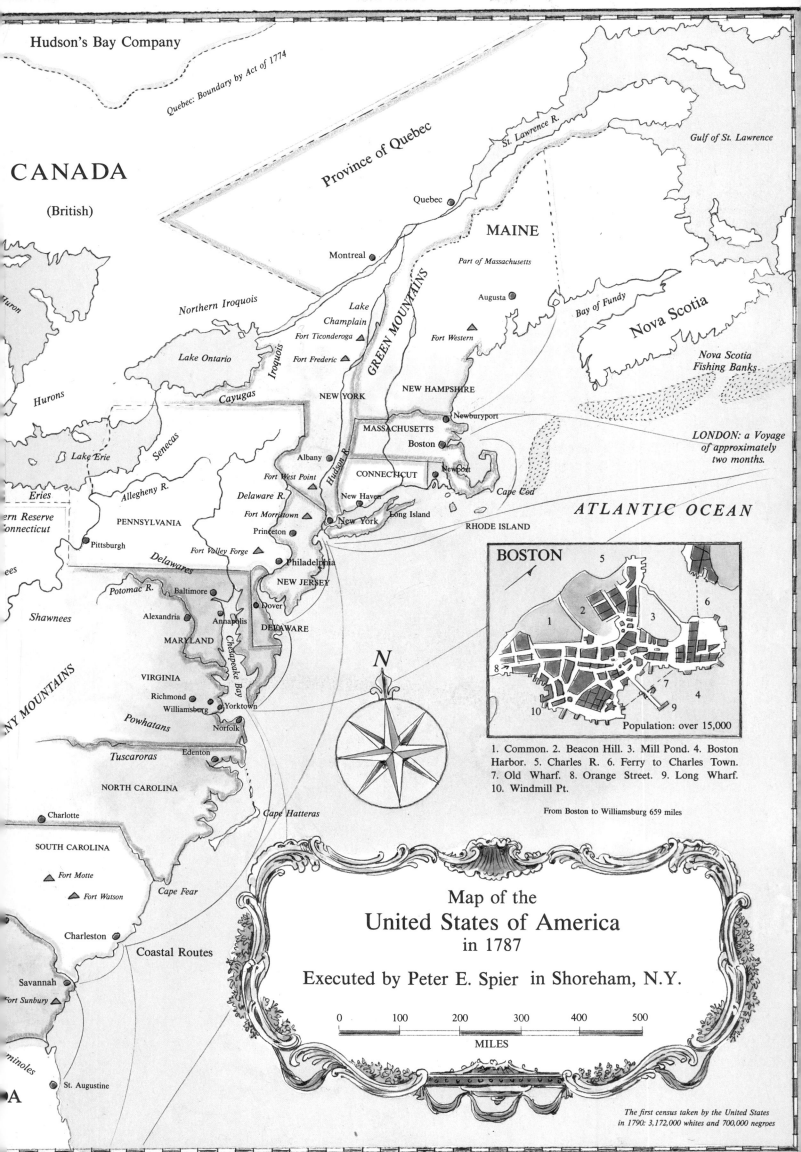

Hudson's Bay Company

Quebec: Boundary by Act of 1774

CANADA

(British)

Province of Quebec

St. Lawrence R.

Gulf of St. Lawrence

Quebec

MAINE

Part of Massachusetts

Montreal

Bay of Fundy

Nova Scotia

Northern Iroquois

Lake Champlain

Augusta

Nova Scotia Fishing Banks

Huron

Fort Ticonderoga △

Fort Western ▲

GREEN MOUNTAINS

Lake Ontario

Fort Frederic △

Hurons

Iroquois

Cayugas

NEW HAMPSHIRE

NEW YORK

MASSACHUSETTS

Newburyport

Senecas

Boston

LONDON: *a Voyage of approximately two months.*

Lake Erie

Albany

Hudson R.

Newport

Eries

Allegheny R.

CONNECTICUT

New Haven

Cape Cod

ATLANTIC OCEAN

ern Reserve onnecticut

Fort West Point △

Delaware R.

New York

Long Island

PENNSYLVANIA

Fort Morristown △

RHODE ISLAND

ees

Pittsburgh

Princeton

Delawares

Fort Valley Forge △

NEW JERSEY

Philadelphia

Potomac R.

Baltimore

Dover

Shawnees

Alexandria

Annapolis

DELAWARE

MARYLAND

Chesapeake Bay

NY MOUNTAINS

VIRGINIA

Richmond

Williamsburg

Yorktown

Powhatans

Norfolk

Tuscaroras

Edenton

NORTH CAROLINA

Charlotte

Cape Hatteras

SOUTH CAROLINA

△ Fort Motte

▲ Fort Watson

Cape Fear

Charleston

Coastal Routes

Savannah

Fort Sunbury ▲

* minoles*

St. Augustine

A

BOSTON

5

2

1

3

6

8

7

10

9

4

Population: over 15,000

1. Common. 2. Beacon Hill. 3. Mill Pond. 4. Boston
Harbor. 5. Charles R. 6. Ferry to Charles Town.
7. Old Wharf. 8. Orange Street. 9. Long Wharf.
10. Windmill Pt.

From Boston to Williamsburg 659 miles

N

Map of the
United States of America
in 1787

Executed by Peter E. Spier in Shoreham, N.Y.

| 0 | 100 | 200 | 300 | 400 | 500 |

MILES

*The first census taken by the United States
in 1790: 3,172,000 whites and 700,000 negroes*

Other books by Peter Spier:

THE FOX WENT OUT ON A CHILLY NIGHT
PETER SPIER'S MOTHER GOOSE LIBRARY
   LONDON BRIDGE IS FALLING DOWN!
   TO MARKET! TO MARKET!
   HURRAH, WE'RE OUTWARD BOUND
   AND SO MY GARDEN GROWS
OF DIKES AND WINDMILLS
THE ERIE CANAL
GOBBLE, GROWL, GRUNT
CRASH! BANG! BOOM!
FAST-SLOW, HIGH-LOW
THE STAR-SPANGLED BANNER
TIN-LIZZIE
NOAH'S ARK
OH, WERE THEY EVER HAPPY!
BORED—NOTHING TO DO!
THE LEGEND OF NEW AMSTERDAM
PEOPLE
PETER SPIER'S VILLAGE BOOKS
   BILL'S SERVICE STATION
   FIREHOUSE
   THE TOY SHOP
   THE PET STORE
   FOOD MARKET
   MY SCHOOL
PETER SPIER'S RAIN
PETER SPIER'S CHRISTMAS
PETER SPIER'S LITTLE BIBLE STORYBOOKS
   THE CREATION
   NOAH
   JONAH
PETER SPIER'S LITTLE ANIMAL BOOKS
   LITTLE CATS
   LITTLE DOGS
   LITTLE DUCKS
   LITTLE RABBITS
THE BOOK OF JONAH
DREAMS

We the People

This book is dedicated to the People
of the United States of America.

We the People

The Constitution of the
United States of America

by Peter Spier

Doubleday & Company, Inc., Garden City, New York

Library of Congress Catalog Card Number 86-24205
ISBN: 0-385-23589-5 Trade 0-385-23789-8 Prebound Text and illustrations copyright © 1987
by Peter Spier All rights reserved Printed in the United States of America First Edition

Together for the last time on September 17, 1787, almost four months after having first met here in convention, and having unanimously elected General George Washington its president, thirty-nine of the fifty-five delegates sign the Constitution. (After a painting by H. C. Christy.)

The year was 1787. The Declaration of Independence had been drafted by Thomas Jefferson eleven years before. It had been six years since the Revolutionary War had come to an end at Yorktown. Only three years had passed since the Treaty of Paris restored peace between Great Britain and the young republic. The United States, with a population of less than one million, was at that time a loose confederation of thirteen independent states governed by their own laws and in many matters often at odds with one another.

Things were not well with the country: a strong central government did not exist; states acted in their own interests, often against those of the country as a whole, taxing, for example, simple essentials such as firewood and vegetables from neighboring states with steep import duties. Large war debts had to be repaid, and states with depleted treasuries printed huge quantities of paper money to do so, creating a devastating inflation.

Tea in some places cost over one hundred dollars a pound—a vast sum in those days. The prices of farm produce rose sharply; tradesmen, merchants, and the holders of state bonds could not in turn pay their debts. Countless farmers lost their land, and their resentment and fury against their states and legislatures had risen to a fever pitch.

States had even come to blows. In 1784 fighting broke out between New York and Vermont over a border dispute. In 1786 armed insurgents, mostly farmers deeply in debt, led by Captain Daniel Shays, a veteran of the war, disrupted court ses-

sions, forced the Massachusetts Supreme Court to adjourn, and almost captured the state arsenal, which was full of muskets. "Shays's Rebellion" was put down with the shedding of blood. Public opinion, however, was so strongly in sympathy with the uprising that the government did not dare execute a single rebel.

It had become clear quite early that the Articles of Confederation, "a league of friendship" adopted by the Continental Congress in 1777 and in force since 1781, were completely insufficient to establish the strong central authority needed, and there was even disturbingly serious talk about installing a military dictatorship as the only way to govern the nation efficiently in the face of the rising tide of discontent and economic chaos. The Congress had no clout and was weak, helpless, and broke.

"Wisdom and good examples are necessary at this time to rescue the political machine from the impending storm," wrote Washington to his fellow Virginian, young James Madison, in 1786. Madison had for years been arguing for the need of a strong national Constitution.

Good sense prevailed and delegates of several states met in convention at Annapolis, Maryland, later that year to discuss solving the nation's horrendous commercial problems.

A report of that meeting was promptly submitted to Congress by Madison and Alexander Hamilton, a brilliant New York lawyer, urging it to convene delegates from every state in order to revise the no longer adequate Articles of Confederation, and after some hemming and hawing the Congress formally summoned the states to a convention. Most already had written their own constitutions, and by 1787 the United States was most fortunate to possess the most experienced body of constitutional writers in the world.

In early spring seventy-four delegates from twelve states were appointed to meet for a Constitutional Convention in Philadelphia's State House, where eleven years previously the Declaration of Independence had been signed.

Only Rhode Island, the smallest state, refused to send its delegation, fearing that it would lose all control over its own affairs to the larger states. But they were not the only ones with reservations. Patrick Henry was unconvinced and leery of Madison's forceful ideas for a central government, which might well curtail the well-established right of individual states.

Even the greatly admired and respected George Washington had to be persuaded to come, since he, too, had grown doubtful of whether national unity could ever be achieved and wondered if the Revolution had failed after all.

Thus on May 14, 1787, only a handful of delegates assembled in Philadelphia, although eventually fifty-five delegates attended. Some of the most prominent statesmen in the country were missing: John Jay was unable to leave the Foreign Office in New York; Adams and Jefferson were away on foreign missions.

But other powerful giants were there: Washington, who had changed his mind; Madison, "father of the Constitution"; Hamilton; Gouverneur Morris of Pennsylvania; and the revered, ailing, eighty-one-year-old Benjamin Franklin, to mention just a few. Delegates kept drifting in, and it took until May 28 to reach the required quorum of seven states. Nineteen delegates never showed up because of lack of sympathy for the business at hand or for personal reasons.

It was an immensely gifted, accomplished, experienced, and worldly group of men, over half of them lawyers. Many had served in colonial and state legislatures or the Congress. Six had signed the Declaration of Independence and five the Articles of Confederation. They were well-educated, well-read, and intimately familiar with the classical and modern schools of political philosophy.

It would be wrong to say that the Constitution's noble ideas were either American or new, for they were based on Greek and Roman political ideals, on the principles of Magna Carta, later British laws, and the philosophies and teachings of Locke, Milton, Rousseau, Montesquieu, and others.

George Washington was unanimously elected presiding officer, and the proceedings were held in

Philadelphia's Independence Hall in 1787, where both the Declaration of Independence and the Constitution were born.

After work the convention delegates often met for meals and informal talk in the City Tavern on Market Street, only two blocks away from Independence Hall, and it was here that they met for a farewell dinner before returning home, their monumental task accomplished. The City Tavern still is a popular eating place in Philadelphia.

secret sessions. No outsiders were allowed in, and the curious were kept at a distance by troops. We owe it to Madison, who kept meticulous records of the proceedings, that we know virtually every detail of the convention, for most delegates honored their pledge of secrecy outside Liberty Hall.

After two weeks of preparations, Edmund Randolph, the governor of Virginia, offered the "Virginia Plan" prepared by his delegation, in which Madison had played an important role. It proposed two houses of a national congress, one elected directly by the people, the other by their state legislators. Each state would be represented according to its population and wealth. The plan was hotly debated.

One week later William Paterson offered the "New Jersey Plan," which was basically a revised edition of the Articles of Confederation and envisioned a national assembly consisting of one house representing the states but not the people, and on June 18 Alexander Hamilton presented his own well-reasoned plan, to a large extent modeled on the British system of government.

The debates were endless, often heated, and always intelligent. Tempers flared, threats and accusations began to fly back and forth, and before the month was out the convention was hopelessly deadlocked between the large and smaller states,

mainly over the issue of numerical representation.

Franklin counseled his fellow delegates that they might be aided and enlightened by daily prayers before each session, but to no avail since the convention did not have the money to pay a preacher . . .

Eventually the "Connecticut Compromise" was adopted, which provided a legislative body of a House of Representatives and a Senate. In the House states would be represented according to their population, in the Senate by equal numbers.

The crisis had passed, and the convention went on to such questions as what powers the new government should be granted, taxation, its organization, how to elect a president, judges, and a Supreme Court. A long list.

In order to have something concrete down on paper a Committee of Detail was appointed to draw up a Constitution draft, and while this was being done the weary delegates took a well-deserved ten-day vacation.

General Washington revisited Valley Forge where, in the winter of 1777, everything had seemed lost. When the delegates reconvened, all was not harmony, for violent arguments flared up over the regulation of commerce, which had been one of the key reasons for the convention, and the equally commercial, moral, and emotional question of slavery. Washington and Madison were among the ten slave-owning delegates. However, as before, a compromise was reached by the worn-out delegates, who were ready to go home after months of intense labor.

The first draft of the Constitution was accepted on August 6, 1787, from which the final version of the document, supervised by the Committee of Style and Arrangement, emerged five weeks later. Gouverneur Morris, a member of this committee who had a way with words, fine-tuned and polished the document, and thereby earned for himself the sobriquet "the man who wrote the Constitution."

On September 15 the Convention ordered the Constitution to be inscribed on parchment, and to be printed in five hundred copies, and two days later the Constitution of the United States was adopted. Yet only thirty-nine delegates were willing to sign. Sixteen adamantly refused.

But this was not the end, for in order to become the law of the land the Constitution had to be ratified by nine states, and that was easier said than done.

The problem was that the fundamental rights of the people had been barely considered at the Convention and were not mentioned in the Constitution at all, since most delegates were convinced that these personal rights were sufficiently safeguarded under the individual state laws. There were two opposing camps, the Federalists in favor of ratification, and the Anti-Federalists opposing it.

Far-seeing Thomas Jefferson, in Paris as Minister to France, which was headed toward its own world-shaking revolution, wrote to Federalist James Madison that a bill of rights was needed and was "what the people are entitled to against every government on earth."

By January 1788 only five states had ratified: Connecticut, Delaware, Georgia, New Jersey, and Pennsylvania. That was not enough, and the key states of Massachusetts, New York, and Virginia would determine the outcome.

Early in February Massachusetts ratified the Constitution by a close vote of 187 to 168, and then only after the Federalists agreed to a list of amendments securing the rights of the people. New Hampshire could not make up its mind, and tiny Rhode Island turned the Constitution down flatly by a margin of 10 to 1 late in March. Maryland, to everyone's surprise, ratified towards the end of April, South Carolina followed in July, as did New Hampshire: the required ninth state.

The Constitution now had become the supreme law of the land, and the United States had truly become a nation.

Madison and Hamilton tirelessly kept up the fight for ratification in Virginia and New York, which, with additional rights amendments, approved the Constitution in June and July of 1788. In November of the following year North Carolina became the twelfth state to ratify after Congress proposed a Bill of Rights, and on May 29, 1790, determined, little Rhode Island made it thirteen. But its vote, even then was 34 to 32.

By December 15, 1791, a quorum of states had also ratified the ten amendments to the Constitution, the Bill of Rights, and the great and noble task begun in Philadelphia four and a half years earlier was triumphantly completed.

The name of the gifted scribe of the embellished Constitution was forgotten until 1937 when, in preparation for the 150th anniversary, someone asked, "Whose hand penned this immortal document?" It took almost two years to discover the

Mount Vernon, George Washington's Virginia home. Here the Mount Vernon Conference was held, the first of many that led to the United States Constitution.

answer: he was Jacob Shallus, clerk of the Pennsylvania House of Delegates.

Whose quill wrote the engrossed Bill of Rights, enshrined in the nation's capital with the Declaration of Independence and the Constitution, is not known to this day.

In 1789, the year George Washington was inaugurated as the first President of the United States, two years after the creation of the Constitution and one year before his death, Benjamin Franklin wrote to a friend, "Our Constitution is in actual operation; everything appears to promise that it will last; but in this world nothing is certain but death and taxes."

As so often before, wise, witty Dr. Franklin, Philadelphia's First Citizen, was right again.

The Declaration of Independence, the Constitution, and the Bill of Rights are on public display in the National Archives Building in Washington, D.C., sealed in helium-filled bronze and glass cases which can be lowered instantly into a shock- and fireproof vault.

We the People of the United States,

in Order to form a more perfect Union,

establish Justice,

insure domestic Tranquility,

provide for the common defence,

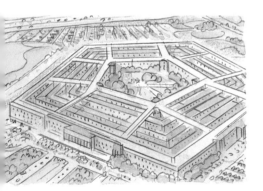

promote the general Welfare,

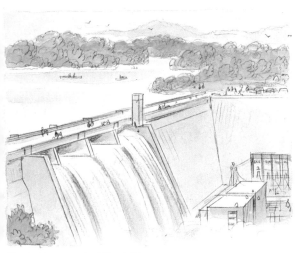

Norris Dam on the Clinch River,
Tennessee Valley Authority

Civil Defense

Veterans Administration

Welcome to the U.S.A.

National Laboratories

Main Reading Room,
Library of Congress

National Wildlife Refuge, Wildlife Protection Agency

Army Corps of Engineers

Air-traffic controllers, Federal Aviation Administration

Public Housing, Dept. of
Housing and Urban Development

Agricultural Research,
Dept. of Agriculture

Nationwide Communications,
Federal Communications Commission

U.S. Mint, Philadelphia, Pennsylvania

National Zoo, Washington, D.C.

National Gallery of Art,
Washington, D.C.

U.S. Weather Service

National Arboretum,
Washington, D.C.

U.S. Public Health Service

Environmental Protection Agency

Smithsonian Air and Space Museum, Washington, D.C.

Grand Teton National Park, Wyoming
8 National Parks

Medicare, Medicaid

an Juan, Puerto Rico
2 National Historic Sites

Glacier Bay, Alaska
12 National Preserves

Gila Cliff Dwellings, New Mexico
77 National Monuments

alley Forge, Pennsylvania
National Historic Parks

Pictured Rocks, Michigan
4 National Lake Shores

Point Reyes, California
10 National Sea Shores

and secure the Blessings of Liberty

Freedom of Religion

Freedom of Speech

Freedom of the Press

The Right to Assemble Peaceably

The Right to Petition

No Search Without Warrant

to ourselves and our Posterity,

▶ Adoption Agencies

done in Convention by the Unanimous Consent of the States present the Seventeenth Day of September in the Year of our Lord one thousand seven hundred and Eighty seven and of the Independance of the United States of America the Twelfth **In Witness** whereof We have hereunto subscribed our Names.

Delaware
Geo: Read
Gunning Bedford jun
John Dickinson
Richard Bassett
Jaco: Broom

Maryland
James McHenry
Dan of St Thos. Jenifer
Danl Carroll

Virginia
John Blair
James Madison Jr.

North Carolina
Wm Blount
Richd. Dobbs Spaight.
Hu Williamson

South Carolina
J. Rutledge
Charles Cotesworth Pinckney
Charles Pinckney
Pierce Butler

Georgia
William Few
Abr Baldwin

G° Washington—Presid.t
and deputy from Virginia

New Hampshire
John Langdon
Nicholas Gilman

Massachusetts
Nathaniel Gorham
Rufus King

Connecticut
Wm Saml Johnson
Roger Sherman

New York
Alexander Hamilton

New Jersey
Wil: Livingston
David Brearley
Wm Paterson
Jona: Dayton

Pennsylvania
B Franklin
Thomas Mifflin
Robt Morris
Geo. Clymer
Thos FitzSimons
Jared Ingersoll
James Wilson
Gouv Morris

The Signers of the Constitution on September 17, 1787, arranged in alphabetical order.

* Signer of the Declaration of Independence. † Signer of the Articles of Confederation.

Abraham Baldwin
1754–1807
For Georgia. Lawyer; minister; founder of Franklin College (University of Georgia).

Richard Bassett
1745–1815
For Delaware. Lawyer; planter-slave owner; governor of Delaware.

Gunning Bedford, Jr.
1747–1812
For Delaware. Lawyer; investor.

John Blair
1732–1800
For Virginia. Lawyer; planter-slave owner; judge; founder and first president of William and Mary College.

William Blount
1749–1800
For North Carolina. Politician; planter-slave owner; land speculator.

David Brearley
1745–90
For New Jersey. Lawyer.

Jacob Broom
1752–1810
For Delaware. Surveyor; banker; manufacturer; postmaster.

Pierce Butler
1744–1822
For South Carolina. Planter-slave owner.

Daniel Carroll†
1730–96
For Maryland. Planter-slave owner; politician.

George Clymer*
1739–1813
For Pennsylvania. Merchant; land speculator; governor.

Jonathan Dayton
1760–1824
For New Jersey. Lawyer; merchant; politician; land speculator; prisoner of war.

John Dickinson
1732–1808
For Delaware. Lawyer; governor; founder of Dickinson College.

William Few
1748–1828
Georgia. Lawyer; soldier;
...

Thomas FitzSimons
1741–1811
For Pennsylvania. Businessman;
land speculator; investor.

Benjamin Franklin*
1706–90
For Pennsylvania. Printer; scientist; philosopher; ambassador;
governor.

Nicholas Gilman
1755–1814
For New Hampshire. Merchant;
soldier.

Nathaniel Gorham
1738–96
For Massachusetts. Merchant;
land speculator.

Alexander Hamilton
1757–1804
For New York. Lawyer; general;
statesman.

Jared Ingersoll
1749–1822
Pennsylvania. Lawyer.

Daniel of St. Thomas
Jenifer 1723–90
For Maryland. Lawyer; politi-
cian; planter-slave owner.

William Samuel
Johnson 1727–1819
For Connecticut. Lawyer; land
speculator; president of Colum-
bia College.

Rufus King
1755–1827
For Massachusetts. Lawyer; merchant; minister to Great Britain.

John Langdon
1741–1819
For New Hampshire. Merchant;
sea captain; shipbuilder; governor; soldier.

William Livingston
1723–90
For New Jersey. Lawyer; general;
governor.

James McHenry
1753–1816
Maryland. Physician; soldier;
...man; prisoner of war.

James Madison, Jr.
1751–1836
For Virginia. Lawyer; slave
owner; Rector, University of Virginia.

Thomas Mifflin
1744–1800
For Pennsylvania. Merchant;
general; governor.

Gouverneur Morris†
1752–1816
For Pennsylvania. Lawyer.

Robert Morris* †
1734–1806
For Pennsylvania. Merchant;
land speculator; investor; governor.

William Paterson
1745–1806
For New Jersey. Lawyer; governor.

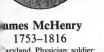

Charles Pinckney
1757–1824
South Carolina. Lawyer;
...r-slave owner; land specu-
...governor; prisoner of war;
...sador to Spain.

Charles Cotesworth
Pinckney 1746–1825
For South Carolina. Lawyer;
planter-slave owner; land speculator; general; prisoner of war;
ambassador to France.

George Read*
1733–98
For Delaware. Lawyer; governor.

John Rutledge
1739–1800
For South Carolina. Lawyer;
planter-slave owner; governor.

Roger Sherman* †
1721–93
For Connecticut. Cobbler; lawyer; land speculator.

Richard D. Spaight,
Jr. 1758–1802
For North Carolina. Planter-
slave owner; politician; governor;
prisoner of war.

George Washington
1732–99
For Virginia. Planter-slave
owner; commander in chief, Continental Army.

Hugh Williamson
1735–1819
For North Carolina. Physician;
merchant; scientist.

James Wilson*
1742–98
For Pennsylvania. Lawyer; merchant; land speculator.

do ordain and establish this Constitution

Grand Canyon, Arizona

"This Is the Place" Monument, Utah

Mount Rushmore, South Dakota

Golden Gate Bridge, San Francisco, California

The Capitol, Williamsburg, Virginia

Plymouth Rock, Massachusetts

Minute Man, Concord, Massachusetts

for the United States of America.

CONSTITUTION OF THE UNITED STATES

We the People of the United States, in Order to form a more perfect Union, establish Justice, insure domestic Tranquility, provide for the common defence, promote the general Welfare, and secure the Blessings of Liberty to ourselves and our Posterity, do ordain and establish this Constitution for the United States of America.

Article. I.

Section. 1. All legislative Powers herein granted shall be vested in a Congress of the United States, which shall consist of a Senate and House of Representatives.

Section. 2. The House of Representatives shall be composed of Members chosen every second Year by the People of the several States, and the Electors in each State shall have the Qualifications requisite for Electors of the most numerous Branch of the State Legislature.

No Person shall be a Representative who shall not have attained to the Age of twenty five Years, and been seven Years a Citizen of the United States, and who shall not, when elected, be an Inhabitant of that State in which he shall be chosen.

[Representatives and [direct Taxes] shall be apportioned among the several States [which may be included within this Union,] according to their respective Numbers, which shall be determined by adding to the whole Number of free Persons, including those bound to Service for a Term of Years, and excluding Indians not taxed, three fifths of all other Persons.][1] The actual Enumeration shall be made within three Years after the first Meeting of the Congress of the United States, and within every subsequent Term of ten Years, in such Manner as they shall by Law direct. The number of Representatives shall not exceed one for every thirty Thousand, but each State shall have at Least one Representative; and until such enumeration shall be made, the State of New Hampshire shall be entitled to chuse three, Massachusetts eight, Rhode-Island and Providence Plantations one, Connecticut five, New-York six, New Jersey four, Pennsylvania eight, Delaware one, Maryland six, Virginia ten, North Carolina five, South Carolina five, and Georgia three.

When vacancies happen in the Representation from any State, the Executive authority thereof shall issue Writs of Election to fill such Vacancies.

The House of Representatives shall chuse their Speaker and other Officers; and shall have the sole Power of Impeachment.

Section. 3. The Senate of the United States shall be composed of two Senators from each State, [chosen by the Legislature thereof,][2] for six Years; and each Senator shall have one Vote.

Immediately after they shall be assembled in Consequence of the first Election, they shall be divided as equally as may be into three Classes. The Seats of the Senators of the first Class shall be vacated at the Expiration of the second Year, of the second Class at the Expiration of the fourth Year, and of the third Class at the Expiration of the sixth Year, so that one third may be chosen every second Year; [and if Vacancies happen by Resignation, or otherwise, during the Recess of the Legislature of any State, the Executive thereof may make temporary Appointments until the next Meeting of the Legislature, which shall then fill such Vacancies.][3]

No Person shall be a Senator who shall not have attained to the Age of thirty Years, and been nine Years a Citizen of the United States, and who shall not, when elected, be an Inhabitant of that State for which he shall be chosen.

The Vice President of the United States shall be President of the Senate, but shall have no Vote, unless they be equally divided.

The Senate shall chuse their other Officers, and also a President pro tempore, in the Absence of the Vice President, or when he shall exercise the Office of United States.

The Senate shall have the sole Power to try all Impeachments. When sitting for that Purpose, they shall be on Oath or Affirmation. When the President of the United States is tried, the Chief Justice shall preside: And no Person shall be convicted without the Concurrence of two thirds of the Members present.

Judgment in Cases of Impeachment shall not extend further than to removal from Office, and disqualification to hold and enjoy any Office of honor, Trust or Profit under the United States: but the Party convicted shall nevertheless be liable and subject to Indictment, Trial, Judgment and Punishment, according to Law.

Section. 4. The Times, Places and Manner of holding Elections for Senators and Representatives, shall be prescribed in each State by the Legislature thereof; but the Congress may at any time by Law make or alter such Regulations, except as to the Places of chusing Senators.

The Congress shall assemble at least once in every Year, and such Meeting shall be on [the first Monday in December,][1] unless they shall by law appoint a different Day.

Section. 5. Each House shall be the Judge of the Elections, Returns and Qualifications of its own Members, and a Majority of each shall constitute a Quorum to do Business; but a smaller Number may adjourn from day to day, and may be authorized to compel the Attendance of absent Members, in such Manner, and under such Penalties as each House may provide.

Each House may determine the Rules of its Proceedings, punish its Members for disorderly Behavior, and, with the Concurrence of two thirds, expel a Member.

Each House shall keep a Journal of its Proceedings, and from time to time publish the same, excepting such Parts as may in their Judgment require Secrecy; and the Yeas and Nays of the Members of either House on any questions shall, at the Desire of one fifth of those Present, be entered on the Journal.

Neither House, during the Session of Congress, shall, without the consent of the other, adjourn for more than three days, nor to any other Place than that in which the two Houses shall be sitting.

Section. 6. The Senators and Representatives shall receive a Compensation for their services, to be ascertained by Law, and paid out of the Treasury of the United States. They shall in all Cases, except Treason, Felony and Breach of the Peace, be privileged from Arrest during their Attendance at the Session of their respective Houses, and in going to and returning from the same; and for any Speech or Debate in either House, they shall not be questioned in any other Place.

No Senator or Representative shall, during the Time for which he was elected, be appointed to any civil Office under the Authority of the United States, which shall have been created, or the Emoluments whereof shall have been encreased during such time; and no Person holding any Office under the United States, shall be a Member of either House during his Continuance in Office.

Section. 7. All Bills for raising Revenue shall originate in the House of Representatives; but the Senate may propose or concur with Amendments as on other Bills.

Every Bill which shall have passed the House of Representatives and the Senate, shall, before it becomes a Law, be presented to the President of the United States; If he approve he shall sign it, but if not he shall return it, with his Objections to that House in which it shall have originated, who shall enter the Objections at large on their Journal, and proceed to reconsider it. If after such Reconsideration two thirds of that House shall agree to pass the Bill, it shall be sent, together with the Objections, to the other House, by which it shall likewise be reconsidered, and if approved by two thirds of that House, it shall become a Law. But in all such Cases the Votes of both Houses shall be determined by Yeas and Nays, and the Names of The Persons voting for and against the Bill shall be entered on the Journal of each House respectively. If any Bill shall not be returned by the President within ten Days (Sundays excepted) after it shall have been presented to him, the Same shall be a Law, in like Manner as if he had signed it, unless the Congress by their Adjournment prevent its Return, in which Case it shall not be a Law.

Every Order, Resolution, or Vote to which the Concurrence of the Senate and House of Representatives may be necessary (except on a question of Adjournment) shall be presented to the President of the United States; and before the Same shall take Effect, shall be approved by him, or being disapproved by him, shall be repassed by two thirds of the Senate and House of Representatives, according to the Rules and Limitations prescribed in the Case of a Bill.

Section. 8. The Congress shall have Power To lay and collect Taxes, Duties, Imposts and Excises, to pay the Debts and provide for the common Defence and general Welfare of the United States; but all Duties, Imposts and Excises shall be uniform throughout the United States;

To borrow Money on the credit of the United States;

To regulate Commerce with foreign Nations and among the several States, and with the Indian Tribes;

To establish an uniform Rule of Naturalization, and uniform Laws on the subject of Bankruptcies throughout the United States;

---

[1] Changed by section 2 of the Fourteenth Amendment.
[2] Changed by section 1 of the Seventeenth Amendment.
[3] Changed by section 2 of the Seventeenth Amendment.

[1] Changed by section 2 of the Twentieth Amendment.

To coin Money, regulate the Value thereof, and of foreign Coin, and fix the Standard of Weights and Measures;

To provide for the Punishment of counterfeiting the Securities and current Coin of the United States;

To establish Post Offices and post Roads;

To promote the Progress of Science and useful Arts, by securing for limited Times to Authors and Inventors the exclusive Right to their respective Writings and Discoveries;

To constitute Tribunals inferior to the supreme Court;

To define and punish Piracies and Felonies committed on the high Seas, and Offenses against the Law of Nations;

To declare War, grant Letters of Marque and Reprisal, and make Rules concerning Captures on Land and Water;

To raise and support Armies, but no Appropriation of Money to that Use shall be for a longer Term than two Years;

To provide and maintain a Navy;

To make Rules for the Government and Regulation of the land and naval Forces;

To provide for calling forth the Militia to execute the Laws of the Union, suppress Insurrections and repel Invasions;

To provide for organizing, arming, and disciplining, the Militia, and for governing such Part of them as may be employed in the Service of the United States, reserving to the States respectively, the Appointment of the Officers, and the Authority of training the Militia according to the discipline prescribed by Congress;

To exercise exclusive Legislation in all Cases whatsoever, over such District (not exceeding ten Miles square) as may, by Cession of particular States, and the Acceptance of Congress, become the Seat of the Government of the United States, and to exercise like Authority over all Places purchased by the Consent of the Legislature of the State in which the Same shall be, for the Erection of Forts, Magazines, Arsenals, dock-Yards and other needful Buildings;—And

To make all Laws which shall be necessary and proper for carrying into Execution the foregoing Powers, and all other Powers vested by this Constitution in the Government of the United States, or in any Department or Officer thereof.

Section. 9. The Migration or Importation of such Persons as any of the States now existing shall think proper to admit, shall not be prohibited by the Congress prior to the Year one thousand eight hundred and eight, but a Tax or duty may be imposed on such Importation, not exceeding ten dollars for each Person.

The Privilege of the Writ of Habeas Corpus shall not be suspended, unless when in Cases of Rebellion or Invasion the public Safety may require it.

No Bill of Attainder or ex post facto Law shall be passed.

No Capitation, or other direct, Tax shall be laid, unless in Proportion to the Census or Enumeration herein before directed to be taken.

No Tax or Duty shall be laid on Articles exported from any State.

No Preference shall be given by any Regulation of Commerce or Revenue to the Ports of one State over those of another: nor shall Vessels bound to, or from, one State, be obliged to enter, clear, or pay Duties in another.

No Money shall be drawn from the Treasury, but in Consequence of Appropriations made by Law; and a regular Statement and Account of the Receipts and Expenditures of all public Money shall be published from time to time.

No Title of Nobility shall be granted by the United States: And no Person holding any Office of Profit or Trust under them, shall, without the Consent of the Congress, accept of any present, Emolument, Office, or Title, of any kind whatever, from any King, Prince, or foreign State.

Section. 10. No State shall enter into any Treaty, Alliance, or Confederation; grant Letters of Marque and Reprisal; coin Money; emit Bills of Credit; make any Thing but gold and silver Coin a Tender in Payment of Debts; pass any Bill of Attainder, ex post facto Law, or Law impairing the Obligation of Contracts, or grant any Title of Nobility.

No State shall, without the Consent of the Congress, lay any Imposts or Duties on Imports or Exports, except what may be absolutely necessary for executing its inspection Laws: and the net Produce of all Duties and Imposts, laid by any State on Imports or Exports, shall be for the Use of the Treasury of the United States; and all such Laws shall be subject to the Revision and Controul of the Congress.

No State shall, without the Consent of Congress, lay any Duty of Tonnage, keep Troops, or Ships of War in time of Peace, enter into any Agreement or Compact with another State, or with a foreign Power, or engage in War, unless actually invaded, or in such imminent Danger as will not admit of delay.

Article. II.

Section. 1. The executive Power shall be vested in a President of the United States of America. He shall hold his Office during the Term of four Years, and, together with the Vice President, chosen for the same Term, be elected, as follows:

Each State shall appoint, in such Manner as the Legislature thereof may direct, a Number of Electors, equal to the whole Number of Senators and Representatives to which the State may be entitled in the Congress: but no Senator or Representative, or Person holding an Office of Trust or Profit under the United States, shall be appointed an Elector.

[The Electors shall meet in their respective States and vote by Ballot for two Persons, of whom one at least shall not be an Inhabitant of the same State with themselves. And they shall make a List of all the Persons voted for, and of the Number of Votes for each; which List they shall sign and certify, and transmit sealed to the Seat of the Government of the United States, directed to the President of the Senate. The President of the Senate shall, in the Presence of the Senate and House of Representatives, open all the Certificates, and the Votes shall then be counted. The Person having the greatest Number of Votes shall be the President, if such Number be a Majority of the whole Number of Electors appointed; and if there be more than one who have such Majority, and have an equal Number of Votes, then the House of Representatives shall immediately chuse by Ballots one of them for President; and if no Person have a Majority, then from the five highest on the List the said House shall in like Manner chuse the President. But in chusing the President, the Votes shall be taken by States, the Representatives from each State having one Vote; A quorum for this Purpose shall consist of a Member or Members from two thirds of the States, and a Majority of all the States shall be necessary to a Choice. In every Case, after the Choice of the President, the Person having the greatest Number of Votes of the Electors shall be the Vice President. But if there should remain two or more who have equal Votes, the Senate shall chuse from them by Ballot the Vice President.][1]

The Congress may determine the Time of chusing the Electors, and the Day on which they shall give their Votes; which Day shall be the same throughout the United States.

No Person except a natural born Citizen, or a Citizen of the United States, at the time of the Adoption of this Constitution, shall be eligible to the Office of the President; neither shall any person be eligible to that Office who shall not have attained to the Age of thirty five Years, and been fourteen Years a Resident within the United States.

[In Case of the Removal of the President from Office, or of his Death, Resignation, or Inability to discharge the Powers and Duties of the said Office, the Same shall devolve on the Vice President, and the Congress may by Law provide for the Case of Removal, Death, Resignation or Inability, both of the President and Vice President, declaring what Officer shall then act as President, and such Officer shall act accordingly, until the Disability be removed, or a President shall be elected.][2]

The President shall, at stated Times, receive for his Services, a Compensation, which shall neither be increased nor diminished during the Period for which he shall have been elected, and he shall not receive within that Period any other Emolument from the United States, or any of them.

Before he enter on the Execution of his Office, he shall take the following Oath or Affirmation: —"I do solemnly swear (or affirm) that I will faithfully execute the Office of President of the United States, and will to the best of my Ability, preserve, protect and defend the Constitution of the United States."

Section. 2. The President shall be Commander in Chief of the Army and Navy of the United States, and of the Militia of the several States, when called into the actual Service of the United States; he may require the Opinion, in writing, of the principal Officer in each of the executive Departments, upon any Subject relating to the Duties of their respective Offices, and he shall have Power to grant Reprieves and Pardons for Offenses against the United States, except in Cases of Impeachment.

He shall have Power, by and with the Advice and Consent of the Senate, to make Treaties, provided two thirds of the Senators present concur; and he shall nominate, and by and with the Advice and Consent of the Senate, shall appoint Ambassadors, other public Ministers and Consuls, Judges of the supreme Court, and all other Officers of the United States, whose Appoint-

[1] Superseded by the Twelfth Amendment.
[2] Modified by the Twenty-Fifth Amendment.

ments are not herein otherwise provided for, and which shall be established by Law: but the Congress may by Law vest the Appointment of such inferior Officers, as they think proper, in the President alone, in the Courts of Law, or in the Heads of Departments.

The President shall have Power to fill up all Vacancies that may happen during the Recess of the Senate, by granting Commissions which shall expire at the End of their next Session.

Section. 3. He shall from time to time give to the Congress Information of the State of the Union, and recommend to their Consideration such Measures as he shall judge necessary and expedient; he may, on extraordinary Occasions, convene both Houses, or either of them, and in Case of Disagreement between them, with Respect to the Time of Adjournment, he may adjourn them to such Time as he shall think proper; he shall receive Ambassadors and other public Ministers; he shall take Care that the Laws be faithfully executed, and shall Commission all the Officers of the United States.

Section. 4. The President, Vice President and all civil Officers of the United States, shall be removed from Office on Impeachment for, and Conviction of, Treason, Bribery, or other high Crimes and Misdemeanors.

Article. III.

Section. 1. The judicial Power of the United States, shall be vested in one supreme Court, and in such inferior Courts as the Congress may from time to time ordain and establish. The Judges, both of the supreme and inferior Courts, shall hold their Offices during good Behaviour, and shall, at stated Times, receive for their Services, a Compensation, which shall not be diminished during their Continuance in Office.

Section. 2. The judicial Power shall extend to all Cases, in Law and Equity, arising under this Constitution, the Laws of the United States, and Treaties made, or which shall be made, under their Authority; to all Cases affecting Ambassadors, other public Ministers and Consuls; to all Cases of admiralty and maritime Jurisdiction; to Controversies to which the United States shall be a Party; to Controversies between two or more States; between a State and Citizens of another State; between Citizens of different States; between Citizens of the same State claiming Lands under Grants of different States, and between a State, or the Citizens thereof, and foreign States, Citizens or Subjects.

In all Cases affecting Ambassadors, other public Ministers and Consuls, and those in which a State shall be Party, the supreme Court shall have original Jurisdiction. In all the other Cases before mentioned, the supreme Court shall have appellate Jurisdiction, both as to Law and Fact, with such Exceptions, and under such Regulations as the Congress shall make.

The Trial of all Crimes, except in Cases of Impeachment; shall be by Jury; and such Trial shall be held in the State where the said Crimes shall have been committed; but when not committed within any State, the Trial shall be such Place or Places as the Congress may by Law have directed.

Section. 3. Treason against the United States, shall consist only in levying War against them, or in adhering to their Enemies, giving them Aid and Comfort. No Person shall be convicted of Treason unless on the Testimony of two Witnesses to the same overt Act, or on Confession in open Court.

The Congress shall have Power to declare the Punishment of Treason, but no Attainder of Treason shall work Corruption of Blood, or Forfeiture except during life of the Person attainted.

Article. IV.

Section. 1. Full Faith and Credit shall be given in each State to the public Acts, Records, and judicial Proceedings of every other State; And the Congress may by general Laws prescribe the Manner in which such Acts, Records and Proceedings shall be proved, and the Effect thereof.

Section. 2. The Citizens of each State shall be entitled to all Privileges and Immunities of Citizens in several States.

A Person charged in any State with Treason, Felony, or other Crime, who shall flee from Justice, and be found in another State, shall on Demand of the executive Authority of the State from which he fled, be delivered up, to be removed to the State having Jurisdiction of the Crime.

[No Person held to Service or Labour in one State, under the Laws thereof, escaping into another, shall, in Consequence of any Law or Regulation therein, be discharged from such Service or Labour, but shall be delivered up on Claim of the Party to whom such Service or Labour may be due.][1]

Section. 3. New States may be admitted by the Congress into this Union; but no new State shall be formed or erected within the Jurisdiction of any other State; nor any State be formed by the Junction of two or more States, or Parts of States, without the Consent of the Legislatures of the States concerned as well as of the Congress.

The Congress shall have Power to dispose of and make all needful Rules and Regulations respecting the Territory or other Property belonging to the United States; and nothing in this Constitution shall be so construed as to Prejudice any Claims of the United States, or of any particular State.

Section. 4. The United States shall guarantee to every State in this Union a Republican Form of Government, and shall protect each of them against Invasion; and on Application of the Legislature, or of the Executive (when the Legislature cannot be convened) against domestic Violence.

Article. V.

The Congress, whenever two thirds of both Houses shall deem it necessary, shall propose Amendments to this Constitution, or, on the Application of the Legislatures of two thirds of the several States, shall call a Convention for proposing Amendments, which, in either Case, shall be valid to all Intents and Purposes, as Part of this Constitution, when ratified by the Legislatures of three fourths of the several States, or by Conventions in three fourths thereof, as the one or the other Mode of Ratification may be proposed by the Congress; Provided that no Amendment which may be made prior to the Year One thousand eight hundred and eight shall in any Manner affect the first and fourth Clauses in the Ninth Section of the first Article; and that no State, without its Consent, shall be deprived of its equal Suffrage in the Senate.

Article. VI.

All Debts contracted and Engagements entered into, before the Adoption of this Constitution, shall be as valid against the United States under this Constitution, as under the Confederation.

This Constitution, and the Laws of the United States which shall be made in Pursuance thereof; and all Treaties made, or which shall be made, under the Authority of the United States, shall be the supreme Law of the Land; and the Judges in every State shall be bound thereby, any Thing in the Constitution or Laws of any State to the Contrary notwithstanding.

The Senators and Representatives before mentioned, and the Members of the several State Legislatures, and all executive and judicial Officers, both of the United States and of the several States, shall be bound by Oath or Affirmation, to support this Constitution; but no religious Test shall ever be required as a Qualification to any Office or public Trust under the United States.

Article. VII.

The Ratification of the Conventions of nine States, shall be sufficient for the Establishment of this Constitution between the States so ratifying the Same.

Done in Convention by the Unanimous Consent of the States present the Seventeenth Day of September in the Year of our Lord one thousand seven hundred and Eighty seven and of the Independence of the United States of America the Twelfth In Witness whereof We have hereunto subscribed our Names,

Go. Washington —Presid.t
and deputy from Virginia

The Word, "the," being interlined between the seventh and eighth Lines of the first Page, The Word "Thirty" being partly written on an Erazure in the fifteenth Line of the first Page, The Words "is tried" being interlined between the thirty second and thirty third Lines of the first Page and the Word "the" being interlined between the forty third and forty fourth Lines of the second Page.

Attest William Jackson Secretary

New Hampshire	(	John Langdon
	(	Nicholas Gilman
Massachusetts	(	Nathaniel Gorham
	(	Rufus King
Connecticut	(	Wm. Saml. Johnson
	(	Roger Sherman
New York	(	Alexander Hamilton
New Jersey	(	Wil: Livingston
	(	David Brearley
	(	Wm. Paterson
	(	Jona: Dayton
Pennsylvania	(	B Franklin
	(	Thomas Mifflin

[1] Superseded by the Thirteenth Amendment.

	(	Robt Morris
	(	Geo. Clymer
	(	Thos. FitzSimons
	(	Jared Ingersoll
	(	James Wilson
	(	Gouv Morris
Delaware	(	Geo: Read
	(	Gunning Bedford jun
	(	John Dickinson
	(	Richard Bassett
	(	Jaco: Broom
Maryland	(	James McHenry
	(	Dan of St Thos. Jenifer
	(	Danl Carroll
Virginia	(	John Blair—
	(	James Madison Jr.
North Carolina	(	Wm. Blount
	(	Richd. Dobbs Spaight
	(	Hu Williamson
South Carolina	(	J. Rutldge
	(	Charles Cotesworth Pinckney
	(	Charles Pinckney
	(	Pierce Butler
Georgia	(	William Few
	(	Abr Baldwin

In Convention Monday, September 17th 1787.
Present
The States of
New Hampshire, Massachusetts, Connecticut, Mr. Hamilton from New York, New Jersey, Pennsylvania, Delaware, Maryland, Virginia, North Carolina, South Carolina and Georgia.

Resolved,
That the preceeding Constitution be laid before the United States in Congress assembled, and that it is the Opinion of this Convention, that it should afterwards be submitted to a Convention of Delegates, People thereof, under the Recommendation of its Legislature, for their Assent and Ratification; and chosen in each State by the People thereof, under the Recommendation of its Legislature, for their Assent and Ratification; and that each Convention assenting to, and ratifying the Same, should give Notice thereof to the United States in Congress assembled. Resolved, That it is the Opinion of this Convention, that as soon as the Conventions of nine states shall have ratified this Constitution, the United States in Congress assembled should fix a Day on which Electors should be appointed by the States which shall have ratified the same, and a Day on which the Electors should assemble to vote for the President, and the Time and Place for commencing Proceedings under this Constitution.

That after such Publication the Electors should be appointed, and the Senators and Representatives elected: That the Electors should meet on the Day fixed for the Election of the President, and should transmit their Votes certified, signed, sealed and directed, as the Constitution requires, to the Secretary of the United States in Congress assembled, that the Senators and Representatives should convene at the Time and Place assigned; that the Senators should appoint a President of the Senate, for the sole Purpose of receiving, opening and counting the Votes for President; and, that after he shall be chosen, the Congress, together with the President, should, without Delay, proceed to execute this Constitution.

By the unanimous Order of the Convention

GO. WASHINGTON—Presid.t

W. JACKSON Secretary.

AMENDMENTS TO THE CONSTITUTION OF THE UNITED STATES OF AMERICA

ARTICLES IN ADDITION TO, AND AMENDMENT OF, THE CONSTITUTION OF THE UNITED STATES OF AMERICA, PROPOSED BY CONGRESS, AND RATIFIED BY THE SEVERAL STATES, PURSUANT TO THE FIFTH ARTICLE OF THE ORIGINAL CONSTITUTION.

Amendment I.[1]

Congress shall make no law respecting an establishment of religion, or prohibiting the free exercise thereof; or abridging the freedom of speech, or of the press, or the right to the people peaceably to assemble, and to petition the Government for a redress of grievances.

Amendment II.

A well regulated Militia, being necessary to the security of a free State, the right of the people to keep and bear Arms, shall not be infringed.

Amendment III.

No Soldier shall, in time of peace be quartered in any house, without the consent of the Owner, nor in time of war, but in a manner to be prescribed by law.

Amendment IV.

The right of the people to be secure in their persons, houses, papers, and effects, against unreasonable searches and seizures, shall not be violated, and no Warrants shall issue, but upon probable cause, supported by Oath or affirmation, and particularly describing the place to be searched, and the persons or things to be seized.

Amendment V.

No person shall be held to answer for a capital, or otherwise infamous crime, unless on a presentment or indictment of a Grand Jury, except in cases arising in the land or naval forces, or in the Militia, when in actual service in time of War or public danger; nor shall any person be subject for the same offence to be twice put in jeopardy of life or limb, nor shall be compelled in any criminal case to be a witness against himself, nor be deprived of life, liberty, or property, without due process of law; nor shall private property be taken for public use without just compensation.

Amendment VI.

In all criminal prosecutions, the accused shall enjoy the right to a speedy and public trial, by an impartial jury of the State and district wherein the crime shall have been committed; which district shall have been previously ascertained by law, and to be informed of the nature and cause of the accusation; to be confronted with the witnesses against him; to have compulsory process for obtaining witnesses in his favor, and to have the assistance of counsel for his defence.

Amendment VII.

In Suits at common law, where the value in controversy shall exceed twenty dollars, the right of trial by jury shall be preserved, and no fact tried by a jury shall be otherwise re-examined in any Court of the United States, than according to the rules of the common law.

Amendment VIII.

Excessive bail shall not be required, nor excessive fines imposed, nor cruel and unusual punishments inflicted.

Amendment IX.

The enumeration in the Constitution of certain rights shall not be construed to deny or disparage others retained by the people.

Amendment X.

The powers not delegated to the United States by the Constitution, nor prohibited by it to the States, are reserved to the States respectively, or to the people.

[1] The first ten Amendments (Bill of Rights) were ratified effective December 15, 1791.

Amendment XI.[1]

The Judicial power of the United States shall not be construed to extend to any suit in law or equity, commenced or prosecuted against one on the United States by Citizens of another State, or by Citizens or Subjects of any Foreign State.

Amendment XII.[2]

The Electors shall meet in their respective states, and vote by ballot for President and Vice President, one of whom, at least, shall not be an inhabitant of the same state with themselves; they shall name in their ballots the person voted for as President, and in name in their distinct ballots the person voted for as Vice President, and they shall make distinct lists of all persons voted for as President, and of all persons voted for as Vice President, and of the number of votes for each, which lists they shall sign and certify, and transmit sealed to the seat of the government of the United States, directed to the President of the Senate; The President of the Senate shall, in the presence of the Senate and House of Representatives, open all the certificates and the votes shall then be counted; The person having the greatest number of votes for President, shall be the President, if such number be a majority of the whole number of Electors appointed; and if no person have such majority, then from the persons having the highest numbers not exceeding three on the list of those voted for as President, the House of Representatives shall choose immediately, by ballot, the President. But in choosing the President, the votes shall be taken by states, the representation from each state having one vote; a quorum for this purpose shall consist of a member or members from two-thirds of the states, and a majority of all the states shall be necessary to a choice. [[And if the House of Representatives shall not choose a President whenever the right of choice shall devolve upon them, before the fourth day of March next following, then the Vice President shall act as President, as in the case of the death or other constitutional disability of the President—]][3]

The person having the greatest number of votes as Vice President, shall be the Vice President, if such number be a majority of the whole number of Electors appointed, and if no person have a majority, then from the two highest numbers on the list, the Senate shall choose the Vice President; a quorum for the purpose shall consist of two-thirds of the whole numbers of Senators, and a majority of the whole number shall be necessary to a choice. But no person constitutionally ineligible to the office of President shall be eligible to that of Vice President of the United States.

Amendment XIII.[4]

Sec. 1. Neither slavery nor involuntary servitude, except as a punishment for crime whereof the party shall have been duly convicted, shall exist within the United States, or any place subject to their jurisdiction.

Sec. 2. Congress shall have power to enforce this article by appropriate legislation.

Amendment XIV.[5]

Sec. 1. All persons born or naturalized in the United States and subject to the jurisdiction thereof, are citizens of the United States and of the State wherein they reside. No State shall make or enforce any law which shall abridge the privileges or immunities of citizens of the United States; nor shall any State deprive any person of life, liberty, or property, without due process of law; nor deny to any person within its jurisdiction the equal protection of the laws.

Sec. 2. Representatives shall be apportioned among the several States according to their respective numbers, counting the whole number of persons in each State, excluding Indians not taxed. But when the right to vote at any election for the choice of electors for President and Vice President of the United States, Representatives in Congress, the Executive and Judicial officers of a State, or the members of the Legislature thereof, is denied to any of the male inhabitant of such State, being twenty-one years of age, and citizens of the United States, or in any way abridged, except for participation in rebellion or other crime, the basis of representation therein shall be reduced in the proportion which the number of such male citizens shall bear to the whole number of male citizens twenty-one years of age in such State.

Sec. 3. No person shall be a Senator or Representative in Congress, or elector of President and Vice President, or hold any office, civil or military, under the United States, or under any State, who, having previously taken an oath, as a member of Congress, or as an officer of the United States, or as a member of any State legislature, or as an executive or judicial officer of any State, to support the Constitution of the United States, shall have engaged in insurrection or rebellion against the same, or given aid or comfort to the enemies thereof. But Congress may by a vote of two-thirds of each House, remove such disability.

Sec. 4. The validity of the public debt of the United States, authorized by law, including debts incurred for payment of pensions and bounties for services in suppressing insurrection or rebellion, shall not be questioned. But neither the United States nor any State shall assume or pay any debt or obligation incurred in aid of insurrection or rebellion against the United States, or any claim for the loss or emancipation of any slave; but all such debts, obligations and claims shall be held illegal and void.

Sec. 5. The Congress shall have power to enforce, by appropriate legislation, the provisions of this article.

Amendment XV.[1]

Sec. 1. The right of citizens of the United States to vote shall not be denied or abridged by the United States or by any State on account of race, color, or previous condition of servitude.

Sec. 2. The Congress shall have power to enforce this article by appropriate legislation.

Amendment XVI.[2]

The Congress shall have power to lay and collect taxes on incomes, from whatever source derived, without apportionment among the several States, and without regard to any census or enumeration.

Amendment XVII.[3]

The Senate of the United States shall be composed of two Senators from each State, elected by the people thereof, for six years; and each Senator shall have one vote. The electors in each State shall have the qualifications requisite for electors of the most numerous branch of the State legislatures.

When vacancies happen in the representation of any State in the Senate, the executive authority of such State shall issue writs of election to fill such vacancies: *Provided,* That the legislature of any State may empower the executive thereof to make temporary appointments until the people fill the vacancies by election as the legislature may direct.

This amendment shall not be so construed as to affect the election or term of any Senator chosen before it becomes valid as part of the Constitution.

Amendment XVIII.[4]

[**Sec. 1.** After one year from the ratification of this article the manufacture, sale, or transportation of intoxicating liquors within, the importation thereof into, or the exportation thereof from the United States and all territory subject to the jurisdiction thereof for beverage purposes is hereby prohibited.

Sec. 2. The Congress and the several States shall have concurrent power to enforce this article by appropriate legislation.

Sec. 3. This article shall be inoperative unless it shall have been ratified as an amendment to the Constitution by the legislatures of the several States, as provided in the Constitution, within seven years from the date of the submission hereof to the States by the Congress.]

Amendment XIX.[5]

The right of citizens of the United States to vote shall not be denied or abridged by the United States or by any State on account of sex.

Congress shall have power to enforce this article by appropriate legislation.

Amendment XX.[6]

Sec. 1. The terms of the President and Vice President shall end at noon on the 20th of January, and the terms of Senators and Representatives at noon on the 3d day of January, of the years in which such terms would have ended if this article had not been ratified; and the terms of their successors shall then begin.

---

[1] The Eleventh Amendment was ratified February 7, 1795.
[2] The Twelfth Amendment was ratified June 15, 1804.
[3] Superseded by section 3 of the Twentieth Amendment.
[4] The Thirteenth Amendment was ratified December 6, 1865.
[5] The Fourteenth Amendment was ratified July 9, 1868.

[1] The Fifteenth Amendment was ratified February 3, 1870.
[2] The Sixteenth Amendment was ratified February 3, 1913.
[3] The Seventeenth Amendment was ratified April 8, 1913.
[4] The Eighteenth Amendment was ratified January 16, 1919. It was repealed by the Twenty-First Amendment, December 5, 1933.
[5] The Nineteenth Amendment was ratified August 18, 1920.
[6] The Twentieth Amendment was ratified January 23, 1933.

Sec. 2. The Congress shall assemble at least once in every year, and such meeting shall begin at noon on the 3d day of January, unless they shall by law appoint a different day.

Sec. 3. If, at the time fixed for the beginning of the term of the President, the President elect shall have died, the Vice President elect shall become President. If a President shall not have been chosen before the time fixed for the beginning of his term, or if the President elect shall have failed to qualify, then the Vice President elect shall act as President until a President shall have qualified; and the Congress may by law provide for the case wherein neither a President elect nor a Vice President elect shall have qualified, declaring who shall then act as President, or the manner in which one who is to act shall be selected, and such person shall act accordingly, until a President or Vice President shall have qualified.

Sec. 4. The Congress may by law provide for the case of the death of any of the persons from whom the House of Representatives may choose a President whenever the right of choice shall have devolved upon them, and for the case of the death of any of the persons from whom the Senate may choose a Vice President whenever the right of choice shall have devolved upon them.

Sec. 5. Sections 1 and 2 shall take effect on the 15th day of October following the ratification of this article.

Sec. 6. This article shall be inoperative unless it shall have been ratified as an amendment to the Constitution by the legislatures of three-fourths of the several States within seven years from the date of its submission.

Amendment XXI.[1]

Sec. 1. The eighteenth article of amendment to the Constitution of the United States is hereby repealed.

Sec. 2. The transportation or importation into any State, Territory, or possession of the United States for delivery or use therein of intoxicating liquors, in violation of the laws thereof, is hereby prohibited.

Sec. 3. This article shall be inoperative unless it shall have been ratified as an amendment to the Constitution by conventions in the several States, as provided in the Constitution, within seven years from the date of the submission hereof to the States by the Congress.

Amendment XXII.[2]

Sec. 1. No person shall be elected to the office of the President more than twice, and no person who has held the office of President, or acted as President, for more than two years of a term to which some other person was elected President shall be elected to the office of the President more than once. But this Article shall not apply to any person holding the office of President when this Article was proposed by the Congress, and shall not prevent any person who may be holding the office of President, or acting as President, during the term within which this Article becomes operative from holding the office of President or acting as President during the remainder of such term.

Sec. 2. This Article shall be inoperative unless it shall have been ratified as an amendment to the Constitution by the legislatures of three-fourths of the several States within seven years from the date of its submission to the States by the Congress.

Amendment XXIII.[3]

Sec. 1. The District constituting the seat of Government of the United States shall appoint in such manner as the Congress may direct:

A number of electors of President and Vice President equal to the whole number of Senators and Representatives in Congress to which the District would be entitled if it were a State, but in no event more than the least populous State; they shall be in addition to those appointed by the States, but they shall be considered, for the purposes of the election of President and Vice President, to be electors appointed by a State; and they shall meet in the District and perform such duties as provided by the twelfth article of amendment.

Sec. 2. The Congress shall have power to enforce this article by appropriate legislation.

Amendment XXIV.[4]

Sec. 1. The right of citizens of the United States to vote in any primary or other election for President or Vice President, for electors for President or Vice President, or for Senator or Representative in Congress, shall not be

[1] The Twenty-First Amendment was ratified December 5, 1933.
[2] The Twenty-Second Amendment was ratified February 27, 1951.
[3] The Twenty-Third Amendment was ratified March 29, 1961.
[4] The Twenty-Fourth Amendment was ratified January 23, 1964.

denied or abridged by the United States or any State by reason of failure to pay any poll tax or other tax.

Sec. 2. The Congress shall have power to enforce this article by appropriate legislation.

Amendment XXV.[1]

Sec. 1. In case of the removal of the President from office or of his death or resignation, the Vice President shall become President.

Sec. 2. Whenever there is a vacancy in the office of the Vice President, the President shall nominate a Vice President who shall take office upon confirmation by a majority vote of both Houses of Congress.

Sec. 3. Whenever the President transmits to the President pro tempore of the Senate and the Speaker of the House of Representatives his written declaration that he is unable to discharge the powers and duties of his office, and until he transmits to them a written declaration to the contrary, such powers and duties shall be discharged by the Vice President as Acting President.

Sec. 4. Whenever the Vice President and a majority of either the principal officers of the executive departments or of such other body as Congress may by law provide, transmit to the President pro tempore of the Senate and the Speaker of the House of Representatives their written declaration that the President is unable to discharge the powers and duties of his office, the Vice President shall immediately assume the powers and duties of the office as Acting President.

Thereafter, when the President transmits to the President pro tempore of the Senate and the Speaker of the House of Representatives his written declaration that no inability exists, he shall resume the powers and duties of his office unless the Vice President and a majority of either the principal officers of the executive department or of such other body as Congress may by law provide, transmit within four days to the President pro tempore of the Senate and the Speaker of the House of Representatives their written declaration that the President is unable to discharge the powers and duties of his office. Thereupon Congress shall decide the issue, assembling within forty-eight hours for that purpose if not in session. If the Congress, within twenty-one days after receipt of the latter written declaration, or, if Congress is not in session, within twenty-one days after Congress is required to assemble, determines by two-thirds vote of both Houses that the President is unable to discharge the powers and duties of his office, the Vice President shall continue to discharge the same as Acting President; otherwise, the President shall resume the powers and duties of his office.

Amendment XXVI.[2]

Sec. 1. The right of citizens of the United States, who are eighteen years of age or older, to vote shall not be denied, or abridged by the United States or by any state on account of age.

Sec. 2. The Congress shall have power to enforce this article by appropriate legislation.

[1] The Twenty-Fifth Amendment was ratified February 23, 1967.
[2] The Twenty-Sixth Amendment was ratified July 1, 1971.

We the People

of the United States, in order to form a more perfect Union, establish Justice, insure domestic Tranquility, provide for the common defence, promote the general Welfare, and secure the Blessings of Liberty to ourselves and our Posterity, do ordain and establish this Constitution for the United States of America.

Article. I.

Section. 1. All legislative Powers herein granted shall be vested in a Congress of the United States, which shall consist of a Senate and House of Representatives.

Section. 2. The House of Representatives shall be composed of Members chosen every second Year by the People of the several States, and the Electors in each State shall have the Qualifications requisite for Electors of the most numerous Branch of the State Legislature.

No Person shall be a Representative who shall not have attained to the Age of twenty five Years, and been seven Years a Citizen of the United States, and who shall not, when elected, be an Inhabitant of that State in which he shall be chosen.

Representatives and direct Taxes shall be apportioned among the several States which may be included within this Union, according to their respective Numbers, which shall be determined by adding to the whole Number of free Persons, including those bound to Service for a Term of Years, and excluding Indians not taxed, three fifths of all other Persons. The actual Enumeration shall be made within three Years after the first Meeting of the Congress of the United States, and within every subsequent Term of ten Years, in such Manner as they shall by Law direct. The Number of Representatives shall not exceed one for every thirty Thousand, but each State shall have at Least one Representative; and until such enumeration shall be made, the State of New Hampshire shall be entitled to chuse three, Massachusetts eight, Rhode Island and Providence Plantations one, Connecticut five, New York six, New Jersey four, Pennsylvania eight, Delaware one, Maryland six, Virginia ten, North Carolina five, South Carolina five, and Georgia three.

When vacancies happen in the Representation from any State, the Executive Authority thereof shall issue Writs of Election to fill such Vacancies.

The House of Representatives shall chuse their Speaker and other Officers; and shall have the sole Power of Impeachment.

Section. 3. The Senate of the United States shall be composed of two Senators from each State, chosen by the Legislature thereof, for six Years; and each Senator shall have one Vote.

Immediately after they shall be assembled in Consequence of the first Election, they shall be divided as equally as may be into three Classes. The Seats of the Senators of the first Class shall be vacated at the Expiration of the second Year, of the second Class at the Expiration of the fourth Year, and of the third Class at the Expiration of the sixth Year, so that one third may be chosen every second Year; and if Vacancies happen by Resignation, or otherwise, during the Recess of the Legislature of any State, the Executive thereof may make temporary Appointments until the next Meeting of the Legislature, which shall then fill such Vacancies.

No Person shall be a Senator who shall not have attained to the Age of thirty Years, and been nine Years a Citizen of the United States, and who shall not, when elected, be an Inhabitant of that State for which he shall be chosen.

The Vice President of the United States shall be President of the Senate, but shall have no Vote, unless they be equally divided.

The Senate shall chuse their other Officers, and also a President pro tempore, in the Absence of the Vice President, or when he shall exercise the Office of President of the United States.

The Senate shall have the sole Power to try all Impeachments. When sitting for that Purpose, they shall be on Oath or Affirmation. When the President of the United States is tried, the Chief Justice shall preside: And no Person shall be convicted without the Concurrence of two thirds of the Members present.

Judgment in Cases of Impeachment shall not extend further than to removal from Office, and disqualification to hold and enjoy any Office of honor, Trust or Profit under the United States: but the Party convicted shall nevertheless be liable and subject to Indictment, Trial, Judgment and Punishment, according to Law.

Section. 4. The Times, Places and Manner of holding Elections for Senators and Representatives, shall be prescribed in each State by the Legislature thereof; but the Congress may at any time by Law make or alter such Regulations, except as to the Places of chusing Senators.

The Congress shall assemble at least once in every Year, and such Meeting shall be on the first Monday in December, unless they shall by Law appoint a different Day.

Section. 5. Each House shall be the Judge of the Elections, Returns and Qualifications of its own Members, and a Majority of each shall constitute a Quorum to do Business; but a smaller Number may adjourn from day to day, and may be authorized to compel the Attendance of absent Members, in such Manner, and under such Penalties as each House may provide.

Each House may determine the Rules of its Proceedings, punish its Members for disorderly Behaviour, and, with the Concurrence of two thirds, expel a Member.

Each House shall keep a Journal of its Proceedings, and from time to time publish the Same, excepting such Parts as may in their Judgment require Secrecy; and the Yeas and Nays of the Members of either House on any question shall, at the Desire of one fifth of those Present, be entered on the Journal.

Neither House, during the Session of Congress, shall, without the Consent of the other, adjourn for more than three days, nor to any other Place than that in which the two Houses shall be sitting.

Section. 6. The Senators and Representatives shall receive a Compensation for their Services, to be ascertained by Law, and paid out of the Treasury of the United States. They shall in all Cases, except Treason, Felony and Breach of the Peace, be privileged from Arrest during their Attendance at the Session of their respective Houses, and in going to and returning from the same; and for any Speech or Debate in either House, they shall not be questioned in any other Place.

No Senator or Representative shall, during the Time for which he was elected, be appointed to any civil Office under the Authority of the United States, which shall have been created, or the Emoluments whereof shall have been encreased during such time; and no Person holding any Office under the United States, shall be a Member of either House during his Continuance in Office.

Section 7. All Bills for raising Revenue shall originate in the House of Representatives; but the Senate may propose or concur with Amendments as on other Bills.

Every Bill which shall have passed the House of Representatives and the Senate shall, before it become a Law, be presented to the President of the United States; If he approve he shall sign it, but if not he shall return it, with his Objections to that House in which it shall have originated, who shall enter the Objections at large on their Journal, and proceed to reconsider it. If after such Reconsideration two thirds of that House shall agree to pass the Bill, it shall be sent, together with the Objections, to the other House, by which it shall likewise be reconsidered, and if approved by two thirds of that House, it shall become a Law. But in all such Cases the Votes of both Houses shall be determined by yeas and Nays, and the Names of the Persons voting for and against the Bill shall be entered on the Journal of each House respectively. If any Bill shall not be returned by the President within ten Days (Sundays excepted) after it shall have been presented to him, the Same shall be a Law, in like Manner as if he had signed it, unless the Congress by their Adjournment prevent its Return, in which Case it shall not be a Law.

Every Order, Resolution, or Vote to which the Concurrence of the Senate and House of Representatives may be necessary (except on a question of Adjournment) shall be presented to the President of the United States; and before the Same shall take Effect, shall be approved by him, or being disapproved by him, shall be repassed by two thirds of the Senate and House of Representatives, according to the Rules and Limitations prescribed in the Case of a Bill.

Section. 8. The Congress shall have Power To lay and collect Taxes, Duties, Imposts and Excises, to pay the Debts and provide for the common Defence and general Welfare of the United ... ... shall be uniform th ... ... States;

In Convention. Monday September 17th 1787.

Present
The States of

New Hampshire, Massachusetts, Connecticut, Mr Hamilton from New York, New Jersey, Pennsylvania, Delaware, Maryland, Virginia, North Carolina, South Carolina and Georgia.

Resolved

That the preceding Constitution be laid before the United States in Congress assembled, and that it is the Opinion of this Convention, that it should afterwards be submitted to a Convention of Delegates, chosen in each State by the People thereof, under the Recommendation of its Legislature, for their Assent and Ratification; and that each Convention assenting to, and ratifying the Same, should give Notice thereof to the United States in Congress assembled.

Resolved, That it is the Opinion of this Convention, that as soon as the Conventions of nine States shall have ratified this Constitution, the United States in Congress assembled should fix a Day on which Electors should be appointed by the States which shall have ratified the same, and a Day on which the Electors should assemble to vote for the President, and the Time and Place for commencing Proceedings under this Constitution. That after such Publication the Electors should be appointed, and the Senators and Representatives elected. That the Electors should meet on the Day fixed for the Election of the President, and should transmit their Votes certified, signed, sealed and directed as the Constitution requires, to the Secretary of the United States in Congress assembled, that the Senators and Representatives should convene at the Time and Place assigned; that the Senators should appoint a President of the Senate, for the sole Purpose of receiving, opening and counting the Votes for President; and, that after he shall be chosen, the Congress, together with the President, should, without Delay, proceed to execute this Constitution.

By the unanimous Order of the Convention

W. Jackson Secretary.

Go: Washington Presidt.

Congress of the United States
begun and held at the City of New-York, on
Wednesday the fourth of March, one thousand seven hundred and eighty nine.

THE Conventions of a number of the States, having at the time of their adopting the Constitution, expressed a desire, in order to prevent misconstruction or abuse of its powers, that further declaratory and restrictive clauses should be added: And as extending the ground of public confidence in the Government, will best ensure the beneficent ends of its institution.

RESOLVED by the Senate and House of Representatives of the United States of America, in Congress assembled, two thirds of both Houses concurring, that the following Articles be proposed to the Legislatures of the several States, as Amendments to the Constitution of the United States, all, or any of which Articles, when ratified by three fourths of the said Legislatures, to be valid to all intents and purposes, as part of the said Constitution; viz.

ARTICLES in addition to, and Amendment of the Constitution of the United States of America, proposed by Congress, and ratified by the Legislatures of the several States, pursuant to the fifth Article of the original Constitution.

Article the first... After the first enumeration required by the first Article of the Constitution, there shall be one Representative for every thirty thousand, until the number shall amount to one hundred, after which the proportion shall be so regulated by Congress, that there shall be not less than one hundred Representatives, nor less than one Representative for every forty thousand persons, until the number of Representatives shall amount to two hundred, after which the proportion shall be so regulated by Congress, that there shall not be less than two hundred Representatives, nor more than one Representative for every fifty thousand persons.

Article the second. No law, varying the compensation for the services of the Senators and Representatives, shall take effect, until an election of Representatives shall have intervened.

Article the third. Congress shall make no law respecting an establishment of religion, or prohibiting the free exercise thereof; or abridging the freedom of speech, or of the press; or the right of the people peaceably to assemble, and to petition the Government for a redress of grievances.

Article the fourth. A well regulated militia, being necessary to the security of a free State, the right of the people to keep and bear arms, shall not be infringed.

Article the fifth. No Soldier shall, in time of peace be quartered in any house, without the consent of the owner, nor in time of war, but in a manner to be prescribed by law.

Article the sixth. The right of the people to be secure in their persons, houses, papers, and effects, against unreasonable searches and seizures, shall not be violated, and no Warrants shall issue, but upon probable cause, supported by oath or affirmation, and particularly describing the place to be searched, and the persons or things to be seized.

Article the seventh. No person shall be held to answer for a capital, or otherwise infamous crime, unless on a presentment or indictment of a Grand Jury, except in cases arising in the land or naval forces, or in the Militia, when in actual service in time of War or public danger; nor shall any person be subject for the same offence to be twice put in jeopardy of life or limb; nor shall be compelled in any criminal case to be a witness against himself, nor be deprived of life, liberty, or property, without due process of law; nor shall private property be taken for public use, without just compensation.

Article the eighth. In all criminal prosecutions, the accused shall enjoy the right to a speedy and public trial, by an impartial jury of the State and district wherein the crime shall have been committed, which district shall have been previously ascertained by law, and to be informed of the nature and cause of the accusation; to be confronted with the witnesses against him; to have compulsory process for obtaining witnesses in his favor, and to have the assistance of counsel for his defence.

Article the ninth. In suits at common law, where the value in controversy shall exceed twenty dollars, the right of trial by jury shall be preserved, and no fact tried by a jury, shall be otherwise re-examined in any court of the United States, than according to the rules of the common law.

Article the tenth. Excessive bail shall not be required, nor excessive fines imposed, nor cruel and unusual punishments inflicted.

Article the eleventh. The enumeration in the Constitution, of certain rights, shall not be construed to deny or disparage others retained by the people.

Article the twelfth. The powers not delegated to the United States by the Constitution, nor prohibited by it to the States, are reserved to the States respectively, or to the people.

Frederick Augustus Muhlenberg Speaker

J 342   24778
SPI
Spier, Peter

We the people

DATE DUE			
OCT 16 1987	11-17 2255		
NOV 7 1987	MAR 2		
APR 9 '91	SEP 2 5		
AP 11 91	10-21		
MAR 31 '92	APR - 5 2014		
MAY 19 '92			
DEC 26 '92			
AUG 20 '93			
JAN 31 '95			
MAR 9 '96			
OCT 16 '97			